ADVANCE PRAISE FOR *R IS FOR REVENGE DRESS*

"A-mazing to 'C' the younger generation B-eing so interested in the legacy of HRH."
—Andrew Morton, author of *New York Times* bestseller *Diana: Her True Story*

"The highly talented royal journalist and broadcaster Kinsey Schofield has produced a stunning tribute to Diana. This book is as beautiful, heart-warming, and inspiring as Diana herself."

—Mark Dolan, GB News

"I is for Icon, and no one knows better than Kinsey Schofield that Diana outshines them all. Evoking more smiles than tears, R is for Revenge Dress captures the fun-loving, carefree, disarmingly human side of the modern era's most celebrated woman. Diana would have loved it."
—Christopher Andersen, author of *New York Times* bestseller *The Day Diana Died*

"The more women who celebrate and talk about Diana, the Princess of Wales, the better! She was an extraordinary, giving, loving woman. I am excited she is being celebrated by Kinsey!"
—Ashley Longshore, artist and author of *I Do Not Cook, I Do Not Clean, I Do Not Fly Commercial* and *Roar! A Collection of Mighty Women*

"With Kinsey's storytelling and illustrations...revenge has never been such fun!"
—Eamonn Holmes OBE, legendary broadcaster and journalist

R is for Revenge Dress

a PRINCESS DIANA–INSPIRED ALPHABET BOOK for GROWN-UPS

KINSEY SCHOFIELD

Post Hill
PRESS

A POST HILL PRESS BOOK
ISBN: 978-1-63758-642-6

R is for Revenge Dress:
A Princess Diana–Inspired Alphabet Book for Grown-Ups
© 2022 by Kinsey Schofield
All Rights Reserved

Cover design by Cody Corcoran

Interior design by Yoni Limor

Post Hill Press
New York • Nashville
posthillpress.com

Published in the United States of America
1 2 3 4 5 6 7 8 9 10

This book is dedicated to Diana, Princess of Wales.

A IS FOR ALTHORP

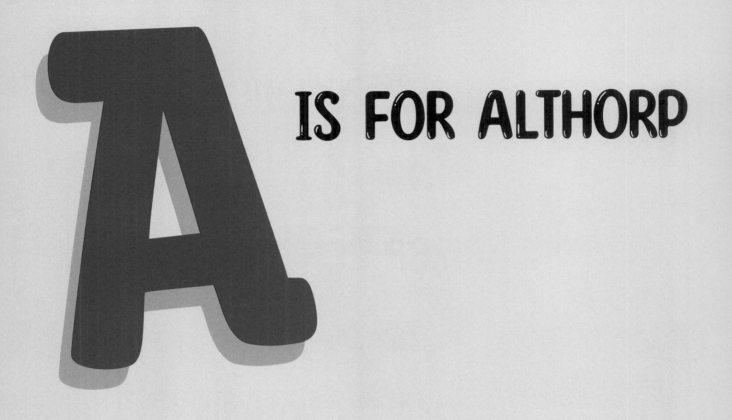

Where it all began.
A prince was coming to visit. A teenage Diana—his fan.
A crush since childhood. She could hardly wait.
This first meeting would lead to a date.

B

IS FOR BLACK SHEEP

This royal rebelled.
On a polo field, her smile hardly held.
The first sign of trouble displayed by a black sheep.
But the lonely princess couldn't make a peep.

C IS FOR CAMILLA

The ex was always there.
Diana heard the whispers and tried not to care.
But her heart was shattered; she wanted her prince.
She had to stop it, and time was of the essence.

D IS FOR DIANA

She was supposed to be a boy.
Her parents took days to name her.
She was an unexpected joy.
Named after the ancient goddess, Diana was strong.
Her life was short, but her legacy lives on.

E IS FOR ENGAGEMENT RING

Diana chose the biggest one.
The most iconic ring in history,
would eventually go to her son.
The Duchess of Cambridge now wears
the sapphire close to her heart.
So Prince William and Princess Diana
are never far apart.

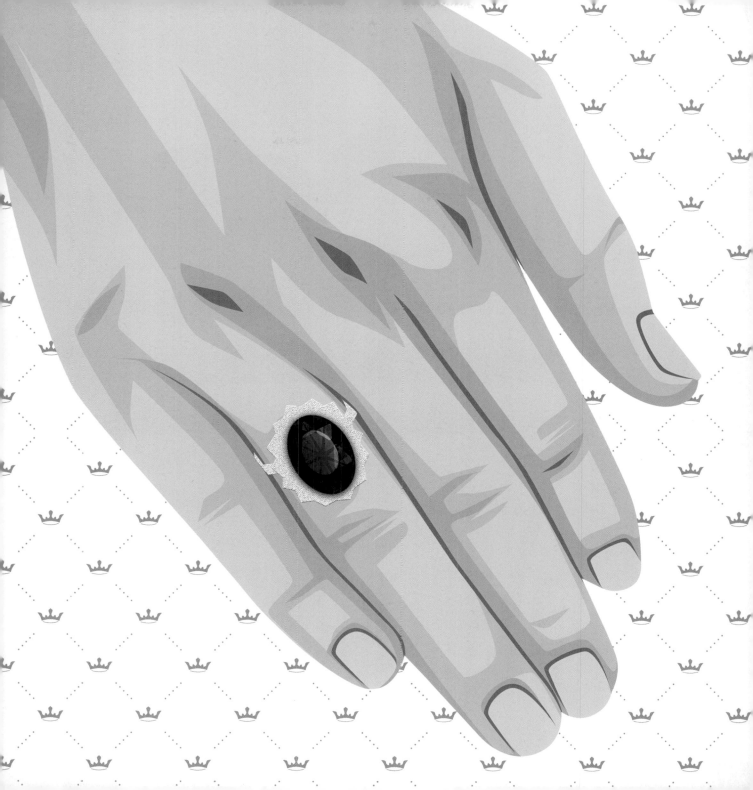

F

IS FOR
FREDDIE MERCURY

Of the legendary Queen.
The two needed a night out
but didn't want to cause a scene.
A night on the town meant a disguise...
and not a single soul recognized
Princess Diana's blue eyes.

G IS FOR GOLDEN GIRLS

A royal's guilty pleasure.
The princess would mute the show
and add her own sense of humor.
Diana's racy ad-libs sent her friends into fits.
Who would ever imagine such naughty words
coming from a princess's lips?

H
IS FOR HARRY AND MEGHAN

Harry is Diana's youngest son.
He found a pretty actress and knew she was the one.
The two moved to America where they raise their kids.
Diana's presence is still felt wherever Harry is.

I IS FOR IVORY TAFFETA

As seen on her wedding dress.
A twenty-five-foot-long train is kind of hard to miss.
Were the ten thousand pearls heavy
as she walked down the aisle?
It didn't matter to Diana as she gave a nervous smile.

J IS FOR JOKER

Everyone says it's true.
That if you spent enough time with Diana...
she was going to prank you.
She once donned a thong
to give her neighbor a fright.
Prince William once retaliated
by snatching her towel with delight.

K IS FOR KENSINGTON PALACE

Princess Diana's address.
She used to suntan in the gardens
and dance until her hair was a mess.
She enjoyed visits from her boys,
who she loved to surprise.
One time Cindy Crawford was waiting.
You should have seen their eyes!

L IS FOR LADY DIANA

An aristocratic title.
Bestowed upon the teenager
after the death of her grandfather.
Her father inherited Althorp
to become the 8th Earl.
Princess Diana was always and forever
her daddy's little girl.

M

IS FOR MOTHER THERESA

A saint and a friend.
The two would pray together until the very end.

N IS FOR NAUGHTY

Can you sense a theme?
Prince Harry loved her defiant streak
and talks of it with glee.
Diana's cheeky motto will never be forgot:
"Be as naughty as you want, just don't get caught."

 **IS FOR OBEY**

But not for this girl.
Diana removed the old-fashioned saying
when she gave marriage a whirl.
The vow was erased before she said, "I will."
Inspiring a tradition that her children carry still.

P

IS FOR PRINCESS

What else could it be?
Perhaps the color pink, which made her so happy!
From polka dots to solids, to fuchsia and blush rose,
Princess Diana's fashion was always on the nose.

Q IS FOR QUEEN OF HEARTS

She remains to this day.
She never thought she would see the crown,
but went along for the ride anyway.
Forever the Queen of Hearts, she will always reign.
A woman with compassion—
the world will never be the same.

R IS FOR REVENGE DRESS

This is my favorite scene.
Charles went on TV to admit
to the whole cheating routine.
A monumental moment overshadowed in a flash...
by a little black dress.
Diana was a smash!

S IS FOR SAME TIME NEXT WEEK

This story is a riot.
A ring on the phone...Diana went quiet.
Prince Charles was calling; he needed the loo.
Could he quickly stop by? What else could he do?
They were separated now but she was feeling sweet.
He used the bathroom and started to flee.
As he left the palace, she chased him with a wink
and yelled at her ex, "Same time next week?"

T IS FOR TRAVOLTA

The ultimate hunk.
The cameras were flashing
as Travolta's heart sunk.
A dance with Diana.
Everyone would stare.
This would be a story
Princess Diana would eagerly share.

U IS FOR UPTOWN GIRL

A not so pleasant routine.
A surprise performance at the Christmas gala
left Prince Charles awfully mean.
Eight curtain calls after her highest kicks....
She faced her husband. He made her sick.
She just wanted to make him proud.
The two left after an ugly row.

V IS FOR VERSACE

Diana was his friend.
He dressed her in couture
but she insisted on paying him.
No freebies for this princess.
Diana paid in full.
And in return, Gianni helped
the princess feel beautiful.

W

IS FOR WILLIAM AND CATHERINE

Cute as can be.
They met in school and dated
for what felt like an eternity.
They were perfect for each other—everyone could see
Patience is what gives this family bliss and prosperity
The oldest of Diana's boys,
William is preparing to become king.
His wife by his side wearing Diana's stunning ring.

X IS FOR X-MAS GIFT

Diana couldn't resist.
A shiny wrapped package
wasn't safe near this princess.
A peek at her presents always gave her a thrill.
Prince William was even rumored
to have inherited the sneaky skill.

 IS FOR YOU

Yes, you. Where to start?
Diana teaches us to lead with our hearts.
Here's a famous quote that she thinks you'll like too:
"Only do what your heart tells you."

Z IS FOR ZEST

The princess lived her life to the extreme.
From walking among landmines
to the royal regime.
Diana was fearless
and chased happiness until the end.
Her heart was so big
that we considered her our friend.

ACKNOWLEDGMENTS

To my ride or Di-s: Liddle, Edie, Bigly, and Roo...I love you.

My family: Chris McClain, Kim Schofield, Michael Schofield, Greyson Schofield, Reece Schofield, Alaric Schofield, Maverick Schofield, and Carolyn and Richard Rothwell. Please consider this mention your Christmas gift.

Andrew Morton, thank you for your kindness and encouragement. I completely understand why Diana chose you to share her secrets with. You continue to reign as my favorite author.

Mark Dolan, thank you for believing in me and for being my friend. You are the king of late-night TV.

Love to Dennis Lynch, Cody Strickland, Nick VinZant, Emili Adame, and my royal watcher friends on Instagram and Twitter! I wish I could fit all of your names on this page. I am lucky to have you in my world!

Finally, thank you so much to Anthony, Maddie, Lisa De Pasquale, and the team at Post Hill Press for this royal opportunity!